LEADER GUIDE: A 7-WEEK STUDY

33 DAYS TO
FREEDOM
FROM
LUST

33 DAYS TO
FREEDOM
FROM
LUST

DR. JARED MOORE

33 Days to Freedom From Lust Leader Guide: A 7-Week Study

Copyright © 2025 by Jared Moore

Published by:
Coram Deo Media

Email: jared@drjaredmoore.com
Website: drjaredmoore.com

Cover design by Jerry Dorris at authorsupport.com

ISBN: 979-8-9937979-3-9

For additional Christian titles, please visit my website at drjaredmoore.com.

CONTENTS

INTRODUCTION

The purpose of this study is to help Christians gain and live in victory in Christ over lust before it takes over their lives and severely harms them and others. By the Holy Spirit through Christ to the Father's glory, they can be freed!

There are several items you need for this Bible study:

- The book *33 Days to Freedom From Lust: A Hope-Filled Devotional* by Dr. Jared Moore, found on Amazon.com.
- The book *The Lust of the Flesh: Thinking Biblically About "Sexual Orientation," Attraction, and Temptation* by Dr. Jared Moore, paperback found at freegracepress.com or the digital on kindle at Amazon.com.
- The Flash drive or YouTube links to the eight 33 Days to Freedom From Lust videos with Dr. Jared Moore, found at drjaredmoore.com.

Each session follows the same structure:

- Getting Started
- Digging Deeper
- Accepting the Challenge

<u>Getting Started</u>: Prayer, discussion, and fellowship.

<u>Digging Deeper</u>: Hearing, believing, receiving, and understanding God's word.

<u>Accepting the Challenge</u>: Applying God's word.

Each week, be sure to encourage your students to enjoy Christ above all things.

After all, the goal of this study is for your hearers to learn how to live in hope with Christ, not in cope with lust.

SESSION 1: UNDERSTANDING LUST, OUR ENEMY

To prepare for your class,

- Read *The Lust of the Flesh*, Chapter 1: "Thinking Biblically About the Lust of the Flesh."
- Watch Video 1: "Introduction."

Main Focus: Romans 8:13; Colossians 3:5

Purpose: To give your group hope, that, by the Holy Spirit within them through faith in Christ to the Father's glory, they can kill the lust in their hearts at the root.

GETTING STARTED

BEGIN by handing out copies of *33 Days to Freedom From Lust: A Hope-Filled Devotional* to your students. Tell them that you will read the "Introduction" and "How to Use This Book" together in a few moments.

THEN, ask your students what they hope to learn and accomplish through this study. Next, take prayer requests, commit to pray for them throughout the week, and encourage each student to be in prayer for one another as well.

DIGGING DEEPER

Jump into the session by watching video 1: "Introduction."

FIRST, play the video. You can access the video from your flash drive or through the YouTube link provided.

THEN, when the video is finished, lead your class in a discussion over what Jared covered. Feel free to come up with your own questions, or consider asking some of the questions below:

> 1. In what ways does Rosaria Butterfield's story illustrate the dangers of viewing inner evil desires as something other than sin?

> 2. How does believing that evil in your heart is not your fault, but that you are a "victim of unchosen realities," hinder you from repenting and killing your sin?

> 3. Why is inner temptation itself the beginning of lust and not merely sinless or neutral temptation?

4. If lust is morally culpable sin, and is not something good or neutral, how should Christians respond to it?

5. How does Jared's illustration about his supervisor and the woman at the sandwich shop show the effects of having an unbiblical understanding of lust?

6. How do the statistics about pornography use among Christians highlight the importance of having a biblical understanding that we are responsible for our lust, even at the root?

7. In what ways does believing in the concept of "sexual orientation" remove personal responsibility?

NEXT, read together the "Introduction" and "How to Use This Book" from *33 Days to Freedom From Lust*. Feel free to come up with your own questions, or consider asking some of the questions below:

1. Did you have a similar upbringing in a church that was largely faithful, like Jared, but that faltered when it came to teaching faithfully about lust?

2. Because Christian men and women still have a sinful nature but it's powerless to control us unless we permit it, is lust unavoidable in this life, or can we kill it through Christ?

3. What does the Bible say about Christians being able to put to death the sins in our hearts, including lust, by the Holy Spirit's power?

4. Why is it important for Christians to develop holy habits and patterns to starve the motions of lust in our hearts?

5. What does it mean to think God's thoughts after Him?

6. How can this devotional's daily structure—prayer, Scripture and reflection, application, marching orders, and prayer—encourage your personal growth in Christ?

7. If you labor to repent from lust and to abstain from it over the next 33 days, how do you think this will help sanctify you, shaping your affections for God and help you form holy habits that lead to greater maturity in Christ for the rest of your life?

ACCEPTING THE CHALLENGE

Focus your group's attention on a few takeaways from your time together.

Ask the group what they think the main takeaways are from this lesson that they can apply to their lives this week. If the following are not mentioned, encourage them to consider these points as well,

1. I am responsible for every evil impulse that springs up in my heart; therefore, I must never make excuses for my sin.

2. Since I am a Christian, by the Holy Spirit, I can repent of lust at the root in my heart.

3. Since I am a Christian, by the Holy Spirit, I can develop holy habits that starve the lust in my heart so much so that it will die and I will no longer give in to it or even struggle with it.

FINALLY, encourage your group to enjoy Jesus above all things this coming week. Tell them to read Days 1-7 in *33 Days to Freedom From Lust* to prepare for your next meeting together, which will be one week from today. Also, encourage them that if they want to further think on the Scripture and theology that they read each day, that they should try to write a poem to summarize what they read, or a poem of response.

Pray and dismiss.

SESSION 2: THE LUST OF THE FLESH WAS MAN'S FIRST SIN

To prepare for your class,

- Read *The Lust of the Flesh*, Chapter 2: "Genesis 3:1-6 – Adam and Eve Willed the Lust of the Flesh."
- Watch Video 2: "Genesis 3:1-6 – Defining Sin."
- Read Days 1-7 of *33 Days to Freedom From Lust*.

Main Focus: Genesis 3:1-6

Purpose: To understand that the first sin in mankind began in the hearts of Adam and Eve.

GETTING STARTED

Kick off your time together by checking in and reviewing what you discussed last session.

FIRST, remind your group that this is a seven-week video series on gaining freedom from lust and living in freedom from lust.

THEN, ask about last week's prayer requests, take any new ones, and commit to pray for them throughout the week. Encourage each student to be in prayer for one another as well.

DIGGING DEEPER

Jump into the session by watching video 2: "Genesis 3:1-6 – Defining Sin."

FIRST, play the video. You can access the video from your flash drive or through the YouTube link provided.

THEN, when the video is finished, lead your class in a discussion over what Jared covered. Feel free to come up with your own questions, or consider asking some of the questions below:

1. How does Eve's belief in the serpent over God show that the source of all sin is unbelief, or a lack of faith in God?

2. How does Eve seeing the forbidden tree as "good for food," when God provided perfect food for her and Adam and said the forbidden tree was not food for them, reveal the lust in her heart?

3. God created Adam and Eve perfectly good, so where did their desire for the forbidden tree come from?

4. What connection is there between Genesis 3:6 and the 10th Commandment (Deut 5:21)?

5. What or who tempted Adam and Eve, the forbidden tree or the serpent? Why is this important?

6. Why can desiring what God forbids never be good or neutral?

7. How does a biblical understanding of Adam's and Eve's first sin show us that evil desires or lusts in our hearts must be repented of at the root, rather than excused, tolerated, or redirected?

NEXT, discuss your group's reading from this past week, Days 1-7 of *33 Days to Freedom From Lust*. Feel free to come up with your own questions, or consider asking some of the questions below:

1. Why does God's eternal nature surpass the temporary and fleeting nature of lust?

2. How does God's holiness expose the emptiness of lust?

3. How does God's sovereign power expose the weakness of lust?

4. How does God's complete knowledge reveal that lust leads only to destruction?

5. How does God's all-presence reveal the limited nature of lust?

6. How does God's unlearned wisdom expose the folly of lust?

7. How does God's justice demand accountability for lust through His word?

ACCEPTING THE CHALLENGE

Focus your group's attention on a few takeaways from your time together.

Ask the group for what they think the main takeaways are from this lesson that they can apply to their lives this week. If the following are not mentioned, encourage them to consider these points as well,

1. Adam and Eve began to sin in their hearts the moment they had any desire for the forbidden tree. I too begin to sin when I desire anything God forbids.

2. Sin is any form of evil in my heart or any lack of righteousness in my heart. I must repent at the first evil impulse in my heart and instead, live in obedience to God's word from my heart.

3. God's goodness exposes the beginning of lust as sin and as the pursuit of the grave; therefore, lust never begins as good or neutral, and only pursuing God's beauty will tear lust from my heart.

FINALLY, encourage your group to enjoy Jesus above all things this coming week. Tell them to read Days 8-14 in *33 Days to Freedom From Lust* to prepare for your next meeting together, which will be one week from today. Also, encourage them that if they want to further think on the Scripture and theology that they read each day, that they should try to write a poem to summarize what they read, or a poem of response.

Pray and dismiss.

SESSION 3: I AM RESPONSIBLE FOR EVERY IMPULSE OF LUST IN MY HEART

To prepare for your class,

- Read *The Lust of the Flesh*, Chapter 3: "Matthew 5:27-30 – Sexual Attraction is Reserved for Marriage."
- Watch Video 3: "Matthew 5:27-30: Any Lust in the Heart is Sin."
- Read Days 8-14 of *33 Days to Freedom From Lust*.

Main Focus: Matthew 5:27-30

Purpose: To understand that I am responsible for any form of lust in my heart.

GETTING STARTED
Kick off your time together by checking in and reviewing what you discussed last session.

FIRST, remind your group that this is a seven-week video series on gaining freedom from lust and living in freedom from lust.

THEN, ask about last week's prayer requests, take any new ones, and commit to pray for them throughout the week. Encourage each student to be in prayer for one another as well.

DIGGING DEEPER

Jump into the session by watching video 3: "Matthew 5:27-30: Any Lust in the Heart is Sin."

FIRST, play the video. You can access the video from your flash drive or through the YouTube link provided.

THEN, when the video is finished, lead your class in a discussion over what Jared covered. Feel free to come up with your own questions, or consider asking some of the questions below:

1. How does Matthew 5:17-20 inform us that Jesus wasn't teaching anything new in Matthew 5:27-30, but was merely correctly preaching the law, contrary to the teachings of the Pharisees?

2. Why is it significant that Jesus fulfills the law through His perfect teaching, thoughts, and actions from His heart?

3. Why does any form of lust in our hearts, from its very beginning, whether an impulse or mindfully chosen, fail to fulfill the law?

4. What is the significance of Jesus' hyperbolic statement that Christians should cut off their body parts that tempt them (Matt 5:29-30; 18:7-9)?

5. How does Jesus telling us that we must deal with our internal temptations radically, show us that we are responsible for and need to repent of even the root of lust in our hearts?

6. By linking the 7th and 10th Commandments, how does Jesus show us that the beginning of lust in our hearts is the seed of lust, and is therefore, sin that we are responsible for?

7. Why does the claim that Jesus is only condemning intentional lust in Matthew 5:27-30, and not "unintentional lust," fall short, considering Mark 13:6 and Mark 13:22?

NEXT, discuss your group's reading from this past week, Days 8-14 of *33 Days to Freedom From Lust*. Feel free to come up with your own questions, or consider asking some of the questions below:

1. How does God's truthfulness reveal lust as a lie from the devil?

2. Why is lust ugly when compared to God and His design?

3. How does God's love reveal that lust is hate?

4. Why does the selfless unity of the Trinity reveal that lust selfishly takes not gives?

5. How does God's unchanging nature expose lust's constant changing and broken promises?

6. How does Jesus being the God Man, and Christians being conformed to His image, expose lust as mirroring Satan?

7. How does Jesus' victory over the serpent encourage us to put our lust to death?

ACCEPTING THE CHALLENGE

Focus your group's attention on a few takeaways from your time together.

Ask the group for what they think the main takeaways are from this lesson that they can apply to their lives this week. If the following are not mentioned, encourage them to consider these points as well,

1. Jesus' perfect righteousness from His heart shows me what God requires in His law, and the righteousness that I have received in Christ through faith.

2. Because I am declared righteous in Christ and He condemns any lust in my heart, I must repent of lust at its first moment and pursue Christ's righteousness instead.

3. Jesus says I must respond drastically to tempting myself; therefore, I must not excuse any lustful impulse in my heart or put myself in situations that I know will be tempting.

FINALLY, encourage your group to enjoy Jesus above all things this coming week. Tell them to read Days 15-21 in *33 Days to Freedom From Lust* to prepare for your next meeting together, which will be one week from today. Also, encourage them that if they want to further think on the Scripture and theology that they read each day, that they should try to write a poem to summarize what they read, or a poem of response.

Pray and dismiss.

SESSION 4: HOMOSEXUALITY IN ONE'S HEART IS SIN

To prepare for your class,

- Read *The Lust of the Flesh*, Chapter 4, "Romans 1:24-27 – Upside-Down Worship Leads to Upside-Down Desires."
- Watch Video 4: "Romans 1:24-27 – Homosexuality in One's Heart is Sin."
- Read Days 15-21 of *33 Days to Freedom From Lust*.

Main Focus: Romans 1:24-27

Purpose: To understand that I am responsible for the evil passions in my heart.

GETTING STARTED

Kick off your time together by checking in and reviewing what you discussed last session.

FIRST, remind your group that this is a seven-week video series on gaining freedom from lust and living in freedom from lust.

THEN, ask about last week's prayer requests, take any new ones, and commit to pray for them throughout the week. Encourage each student to be in prayer for one another as well.

DIGGING DEEPER

Jump into the session by watching video 4: "Romans 1:24-27 — Homosexuality in One's Heart is Sin."

FIRST, play the video. You can access the video from your flash drive or through the YouTube link provided.

THEN, when the video is finished, lead your class in a discussion over what Jared covered. Feel free to come up with your own questions, or consider asking some of the questions below:

1. What does Paul mean when he writes that "God gave them up in the lusts of their hearts to impurity?"

2. What dishonorable passions does God condemn in Romans 1:26-27, and why?

3. Why would worshipping the creature lead sinners to twist God's creation?

4. Why does Paul mention the women before the men when discussing unnatural relations?

5. What are relations that are "contrary to nature," and why do they oppose nature?

6. If an evil impulse is "unwanted," is it sinless, or are we responsible for it?

7. If worshipping the creature leads to the sins in Romans 1:24-32, what outcomes follow worshipping the Creator?

NEXT, discuss your group's reading from this past week, Days 15-21 of *33 Days to Freedom From Lust*. Feel free to come up with your own questions, or consider asking some of the questions below:

1. How does the prophets longing for Jesus, not lust, encourage us to mortify our lust?

2. How does Israel and David longing for Jesus, not lust, encourage us to mortify our lust?

3. How does Jesus as the true Prophet call us to obey Him rather than lust?

4. How does Jesus' intercession as the true High Priest encourage us to go to Him rather than to lust?

5. How does Jesus' righteous rule as King of kings encourage us to submit to Him rather than lust?

6. Why does Jesus' Lordship and salvation deliver me from the harm and deception of lust?

7. Why does the Holy Spirit's indwelling of Christians empower us to repent of lust?

ACCEPTING THE CHALLENGE

Focus your group's attention on a few takeaways from your time together.

Ask the group for what they think the main takeaways are from this lesson that they can apply to their lives this week. If the following are not mentioned, encourage them to consider these points as well,

1. God made everyone male or female and included in being male or female is pursuing an opposite-sex Christian to marry, unless I have the gift of singleness, so that I may be more devoted to the Lord.

2. Worshipping God every day, by the Spirit through the Son to the Father, in all that I think and do, causes me to lust less, and to become more like Jesus.

3. The key to my faith, repentance, and holiness, is not to think on or talk constantly about myself, but to talk about and think on God and His goodness, truth, and beauty.

FINALLY, encourage your group to enjoy Jesus above all things this coming week. Tell them to read Days 22-28 in *33 Days to Freedom From Lust* to prepare for your next meeting together, which will be one week from today. Also, encourage them that if they want to further think on the Scripture and theology that they read each day, that they should try to write a poem to summarize what they read, or a poem of response.

Pray and dismiss.

SESSION 5: ALL MY SIN BEGINS AS THE LUST OF MY FLESH

To prepare for your class,

- Read *The Lust of the Flesh*, Chapter 5: "James 1:13-15 – We Desire What we are and we are What we Desire."
- Watch Video 5: James 1:13-15 – "To Desire Sin is Inner Temptation and Sin."
- Read Days 22-28 of *33 Days to Freedom From Lust*.

Main Focus: James 1:13-15

Purpose: To understand that sin begins as lust and inner temptation in my heart, then proceeds to mindful sin, and grows into death; and that I must repent of lust at the root so that it doesn't proceed to further harm myself and others.

GETTING STARTED

Kick off your time together by checking in and reviewing what you discussed last session.

FIRST, remind your group that this is a seven-week video series on gaining freedom from lust and living in freedom from lust.

THEN, ask about last week's prayer requests, take any new ones, and commit to pray for them throughout the week. Encourage each student to be in prayer for one another as well.

DIGGING DEEPER

Jump into the session by watching video 5: James 1:13-15 — "To Desire Sin is Inner Temptation and Sin."

FIRST, play the video. You can access the video from your flash drive or through the YouTube link provided.

THEN, when the video is finished, lead your class in a discussion over what Jared covered. Feel free to come up with your own questions, or consider asking some of the questions below:

1. Why are tests and trials good for Christians (James 1:2-4)?

2. Why can't God be tempted or tempt others (James 1:13, 16-18)?

3. What metaphor does James use to describe the life-cycle of sin?

4. If the devil tempts someone, he sins. If we tempt someone else, we sin. If someone tempts us, he sins. But, if we tempt ourselves internally, do we sin?

5. How does James 4:1-10 help us rightly interpret James 1:13-15?

6. Since internal temptation never comes from God, and begins in our hearts, who is always responsible for it?

7. How do internal temptation, mindfully conceived sin, and death share the same nature while one is worse than the other?

NEXT, discuss your group's reading from this week, Days 22-28 of *33 Days to Freedom From Lust*. Feel free to come up with your own questions, or consider asking some of the questions below:

1. How does the Holy Spirit's sanctifying work transform us to love God, and to hate lust?

2. How does the Holy Spirit enable us to overcome lust, which immerses us in sin and death?

3. How does dwelling on lust make us reflect Satan more than Christ?

4. How does lust devalue our bodies and other image-bearers created for God's glory?

5. Why do tempters and pornography, as tools for lust, lead us toward spiritual death and separation from God?

6. How does lust pervert God's design for marriage and singleness?

7. How does lust hide God's glory and deny His wisdom?

ACCEPTING THE CHALLENGE

Focus your group's attention on a few takeaways from your time together.

Ask the group for what they think the main takeaways are from this lesson that they can apply to their lives this week. If the following are not mentioned, encourage them to consider these points as well,

1. When my flesh tempts me, I begin to sin.

2. When my flesh tempts me, and I reject it, I should rejoice, and I should also confess the sin of having wanted something evil, if even for a moment.

3. By calling inner temptation sin, I starve my flesh, and begin to kill it, so that it can never harm me or come out and harm others.

FINALLY, encourage your group to enjoy Jesus above all things this coming week. Tell them to read Days 29-33 of *33 Days to Freedom From Lust*; and to read the Shorter Catechism 1-16 each day for 2 days, to prepare for your next meeting together, which will be one week from today. Also, encourage them that if they want to further think on the Scripture and theology that they read each day, that they should try to write a poem to summarize what they read, or a poem of response.

Pray and dismiss.

SESSION 6: THERE ARE TWO FORMS OF TEMPTATION

To prepare for your class,

- Read *The Lust of the Flesh*, Chapter 6: "Since Jesus was Tempted Without Sin, is Fleshly Desire Still Sin?"
- Watch Video 6: "When we are and are not Tempted Like Jesus."
- Read Days 29-33 and 1-16 of the Shorter Catechism of *33 Days to Freedom From Lust*.

Main Focus: Matthew 4:1-11; 26:36-46; 27:45-46; Hebrews 4:15

Purpose: To understand that there are two forms of temptation: inner temptation, which is lust and always sin, and outer temptation, a good thing offered through an evil means, the way Jesus was tempted, which is only sin if I submit to the evil means.

GETTING STARTED
Kick off your time together by checking in and reviewing what you discussed last session.

FIRST, remind your group that this is a seven-week video series on gaining freedom from lust and living in freedom from lust.

THEN, ask about last week's prayer requests, take any new ones, and commit to pray for them throughout the week. Encourage each student to be in prayer for one another as well.

DIGGING DEEPER

Jump into the session by watching video 6: "When we are and are not Tempted Like Jesus."

FIRST, play the video. You can access the video from your flash drive or through the YouTube link provided.

THEN, when the video is finished, lead your class in a discussion over what Jared covered. Feel free to come up with your own questions, or consider asking some of the questions below:

1. Is temptation ever sin? Why or why not?

2. In Matthew 4:1-11, why did the devil only tempt Jesus with inherently good things?

3. Did Jesus ever desire to disobey His Father, including in the Garden of Gethsemane (Luke 22:42)? Why?

4. Did Jesus doubt God on the cross when He cried out, "My God, My God, Why have you forsaken Me" (Matt 27:46)? Why?

5. What are the two forms of temptation? Give examples.

6. Was Jesus ever internally tempted? Why?

7. When are we tempted like Jesus, and when are we tempted like David or Peter?

NEXT, discuss your group's reading from this week, Days 29-33 and 2 Days of the Shorter Catechism 1-16, of *33 Days to Freedom From Lust*. Feel free to come up with your own questions, or consider asking some of the questions below:

1. How does Christ's beauty draw me to Him, and away from lust?

2. How does my identity in Christ empower me to flee lust and to live for Him?

3. Who is responsible for my lust?

4. How has God equipped me to grow in His virtues and repent of lust?

5. How are pornography and adulterous tempters like serial killers?

6. Why does lust not only speak ill of me but of God as well?

7. Why can lust never satisfy me?

ACCEPTING THE CHALLENGE

Focus your group's attention on a few takeaways from your time together.

Ask the group for what they think the main takeaways are from this lesson that they can apply to their lives this week. If the following are not mentioned, encourage them to consider these points as well,

1. There are two forms of temptation, from within and from without. Temptation from within is always the beginning of sin, and temptation from without is only sin if I desire the evil means.

2. Jesus was only tempted from without, and He never desired the evil means, for He was only tempted by good things that were designed by and only belonged to His Father.

3. When I am tempted from within, I am responsible and must repent. When I am tempted from without by good things offered through evil means, and I reject the evil means,

I have been tempted like Jesus and have not even begun to sin.

FINALLY, encourage your group to enjoy Jesus above all things this coming week. Tell them to read the Shorter Catechism 1-16, each day for 3 days, and the Shorter Catechism 17-33, each day for 4 days, of *33 Days to Freedom From Lust* to prepare for your next meeting together, which will be one week from today. Also, encourage them that if they want to further think on the Scripture and theology that they read each day, that they should try to write a poem to summarize what they read, or a poem of response.

Pray and dismiss.

SESSION 7: AUGUSINTE'S AND THE REFORMERS' TEACHINGS ON LUST

To prepare for your class,

- Read *The Lust of the Flesh*, Chapter 7: "Augustine and the Reformers Versus the Roman Catholic Church," and Chapter 8: "Codifying and Spreading the Reformation Tradition."
- Watch Video 7: "The Great Tradition's Teachings on Lust."
- Read 1-33 of the Shorter Catechism of *33 Days to Freedom From Lust*.

Main Focus: Augustine's and Reformation history's teachings on lust.

Purpose: To understand that Christians have always taught that the beginning of lust in our hearts is the beginning of sin; it is not neutral or good, and we are responsible for it.

GETTING STARTED

Kick off your time together by checking in and reviewing what you discussed last session.

FIRST, remind your group that this is a seven-week video series on gaining freedom from lust and living in freedom from lust.

THEN, ask about last week's prayer requests, take any new ones, and commit to pray for them throughout the week. Encourage each student to be in prayer for one another as well.

DIGGING DEEPER

Jump into the session by watching video 7: "The Great Tradition's Teachings on Lust."

FIRST, play the video. You can access the video from your flash drive or through the YouTube link provided.

THEN, when the video is finished, lead your class in a discussion over what Jared covered. Feel free to come up with your own questions, or consider asking some of the questions below:

1. How does Augustine define the lust of the flesh in his works, and why does he argue that it is not neutral but is sin that we are responsible for?

2. In Ulrich Zwingli's 1523 confession, how did he argue that evil desire is sin before the act, and what role does God's view of our hearts play in this?

3. How does Martin Luther's understanding of the 9th and 10th Commandments show that he believed evil impulses and desires are sins that we're responsible for?

4. In John Calvin's 1541 catechism, how does he explain that even the least inner temptation or evil affection is sin, and what does this say about God's requirement for inward purity?

5. Why does the Heidelberg Catechism forbid even the least impulse against God's commandments, and how does Zacharias Ursinus expand on this in his commentary?

6. How does the Westminster Confession affirm that all motions from original sin in Christians are "truly and properly sin," and what Scriptures does it reference?

7. How did men like Jonathan Edwards, Charles Hodge, and Charles Spurgeon maintain the view that evil impulses in our hearts are sin that we're responsible for?

NEXT, discuss your group's reading from this week, 3 Days of the Shorter Catechism 1-16 and 4 Days of the Shorter Catechism

17-33, in *33 Days to Freedom From Lust*. Feel free to come up with your own questions, or consider asking some of the questions below:

1. In what ways does the serpent's role in the origin of lust highlight its finite beginnings compared to God's timeless self-existence?

2. How might understanding lust's end in the Lake of Fire influence a believer's motivation to repent of it at the root in light of God's everlasting nature?

3. How does God's sovereign power as Creator demonstrate lust's lack of inherent authority over Christians?

4. In what ways does God's unlearned wisdom expose lust as a perversion leading to death?

5. How does God's beauty and the beauty of His design expose lust as ugly and as the pursuit of ugliness, which makes those who pursue it grow uglier?

6. Since God is love, how does His loving nature reveal lust as hatred toward Him, us, and others?

7. How does the longing for Christ of Noah, Abraham, Moses, David, Israel, and the prophets show us His priceless value and the worthlessness of lust?

ACCEPTING THE CHALLENGE

Focus your group's attention on a few takeaways from your time together.

Ask the group for what they think the main takeaways are from this lesson that they can apply to their lives this week. If the following are not mentioned, encourage them to consider these points as well,

1. Throughout history, Christians taught that all sin begins in our hearts as evil impulses of sin that we're morally responsible for.

2. Lust within me is produced by my flesh and starts out as an evil impulse of sin.

3. Only Jesus can give me victory over my indwelling lust; therefore, I must go to Him continually through faith and repent of all that is contrary to Him in my heart.

FINALLY, encourage your group to enjoy Jesus above all things this coming week. Tell them to read the Larger Catechism 1-17 each day, of *33 Days to Freedom From Lust,* to prepare for your next meeting together, which will be one week from today. Also, encourage them that if they want to further think on the Scripture and theology that they read each day, that they should try to write a poem to summarize what they read, or a poem of response.

Pray and dismiss.

SESSION 8: HOW TO FIGHT AND REPENT OF INDWELLING SIN

To prepare for your class,

- Read *The Lust of the Flesh*, Chapter 9: "The lust of the Flesh Cannot be Sublimated to Holiness" and Chapter 10: "Only God-Designed Desires can Lead to Holiness."
- Watch Video 8: "Excuses Cannot Save us From Lust, but Jesus Can."
- Read 1-16 of the Larger Catechism of *33 Days to Freedom From Lust*.

Main Focus: Romans 7:7-25; Galatians 5:16-26

Purpose: To understand that if the beginning of lust in our hearts is not sin, the beginning of anything evil in our hearts is not sin either; and, how to overcome lust and all other sin produced by one's flesh through repenting and believing in Christ, and living His morals.

GETTING STARTED

Kick off your time together by checking in and reviewing what you discussed last session.

FIRST, remind your group that this is a seven-week video series on gaining freedom from lust and living in freedom from lust.

THEN, ask about last week's prayer requests, take any new ones, and commit to pray for them throughout the week. Encourage each student to be in prayer for one another as well.

DIGGING DEEPER

Jump into the session by watching video 8: "Excuses Cannot Save us From Lust. Only Jesus Can."

FIRST, play the video. You can access the video from your flash drive or through the YouTube link provided.

THEN, when the video is finished, lead your class in a discussion over what Jared covered. Feel free to come up with your own questions, or consider asking some of the questions below:

    1. Why can lust never be aimed at God or holiness?

    2. Why does lust never begin as holy or neutral?

3. Why can holiness never become lust, and lust can never become holiness?

4. Why is being born again through repentance and faith in Christ essential to living holy lives from our hearts?

5. How does praying without ceasing and reading, receiving, believing, singing, and memorizing God's word help us to fight against lust?

6. How does consistently worshipping with other Christians in a local church help us fight against lust?

7. How do our pop culture choices shape our affections for good or for ill?

NEXT, discuss your group's reading from this week, Larger Catechism 1-17, of *33 Days to Freedom From Lust*. Feel free to come up with your own questions, or consider asking some of the questions below:

1. How was Jesus like Moses, and different from and greater than Moses?

2. How does Jesus being the King who leads us in righteousness encourage us to repent of giving ourselves to lust, a counterfeit king of evil?

3. Why does thinking on Christ make us more holy, and dwelling on lust make us more sinful?

4. Why does Solomon liken adulterous women, which includes pornography, to serial killers that stalk, prey on, and murder foolish men?

5. How does the logical selfless giving and receiving among the Trinity—The Father begetting the Son, the Son begotten from the Father, and the Holy Spirit proceeding from the Father and the Son—encourage us to reject the selfishness of lust and its exploitive taking from others?

6. How does the Bible from the beginning tie marriage to all humanity being created as male or female, which is ultimately fulfilled in Christ's eternal marriage to His church, and how is singleness for God's glory the exception to this rule?

7. How does Christ looking at us in the same way that He looked at Peter when he sinned, melt our hearts to spur us to repent and worship Him with our whole hearts, souls, and minds?

ACCEPTING THE CHALLENGE

Focus your group's attention on a few takeaways from your time together.

Ask the group for what they think the main takeaways are from this lesson that they can apply to their lives this week. If the following are not mentioned, encourage them to consider these points as well,

1. I will never gain victory over lust if I make excuses for it.

2. I will never gain victory over lust if I never repent of it at the root.

3. Jesus, because His value is infinite, is worth repenting of everything in me that is contrary to Him and His morals. No other human being has loved me or ever will love me like Jesus does. He will finish what He started in me.

FINALLY, encourage your group to enjoy Jesus above all things this coming week. Since this is your final meeting together, give them your final marching orders:

1. This coming week, read the Larger Catechism 18-33, each day. Work to memorize it.

2. In the coming weeks and months, as needed, continue to shape your affections to Christ instead of lust and sin, through listening to the songs and memorizing the Shorter and Larger Catechisms in *33 Days to Freedom From Lust*.

3. In the coming weeks, months, and years, follow these steps to continue to shape and mature your affections toward Christ:

- Consistently worship with other believers in a local church.
- Enjoy Christian community and fellowship.
- Memorize and sing Scripture often.
- Pursue discipleship through reading and studying God's word every day.
- Pursue accountability to other believers.
- Make pop culture choices that point you to God's good, truth, and beauty.
- Rest in Christ, because He has saved you eternally by taking your sin away and giving you His righteousness. Therefore, get up and live His morals from your heart.

Pray and Dismiss.

Other Books by Dr. Jared Moore

1. You can read my articles and books as I write them, weekly, at my Substack[1] or Patreon[2] at "Dr. Jared Moore."

2. *The Lust of the Flesh: Thinking Biblically About "Sexual Orientation," Attraction, and Temptation.* Published by Free Grace Press.

3. *Same-Sex Attraction and the Temptation of Christ.* Published by Founders.

4. Co-author of *The Pop Culture Parent: Helping Kids Engage Their World for Christ.* Published by New Growth Press.

5. *A Biblical and Historical Appraisal of Concupiscence with Special Attention to Same-Sex Attraction.* Published by Southern Baptist Theological Seminary.

---

[1] https://drjaredmoore.com/.
[2] https://www.patreon.com/c/u16977519.

Other Books by Dr. Jared Moore